JUST DO YOUR BEST

A CONCISE, COMPLETE GUIDE TO
ON-THE-JOB SUCCESS

D0032737

By Chuck Harwood
With Elaine de Man

Group Fore Productions, Inc.
Menlo Park, California
2006

Just Do Your Best

Printed in U.S.A.

ISBN 0-88197-101-4

Group Fore Productions
1259 El Camino Real, Suite 153
Menlo Park, California 94025
(650) 327-5207
FAX (650) 327-5208
www.JustDoYourBest.com

PREFACE

You no doubt already have a collection of guidebooks lying around your home. They probably cover such things as dieting, cooking, repairing things, bird watching, travel, personal improvement, and computing, just to name a few. But I'll bet you don't have a guidebook that covers perhaps the most important thing you do—your job, your livelihood. And even if you do, it's probably neither concise nor complete nor a size you can carry around in your purse or pocket. But that is precisely what you are holding in your hand right now—a simple, concise guidebook that covers the fundamentals of everything you need to know about how to do the best you can at what you do for a living—whatever it is.

Whether you work in the mailroom or the boardroom, whether you are a shopkeeper or a real estate tycoon, this book applies to you. How can I make such an overarching generalization? It's easy. I contend that the content of all work, and I mean *all* work, can be broken down into five component parts: **knowing, deciding, assigning, influencing,** and **coping.** In order to be truly successful at your job and to enjoy all the consequent rewards, all you need to do is identify these five components in the job you do and master each and every one of them. And that's all there really is to it.

Having said that, I should add that simply reading the book is not enough. You must apply what you have learned and make sure you are competent in all five parts of your work. Compare it to your automobile. You may have bought it because you liked the way it looked, how it felt, and how it handled. But if the engine misses, or the windows leak, or the brakes squeal, or the wipers fail, or the radio squawks, or the tires wobble, you've got a lemon. All the parts have to be working properly, and the same goes for you and your work.

The second key to your on-the-job success is to understand that no one else is going to do this for you. You, and you alone, are responsible for your future. Plenty of people will have suggestions—your boss, your peers, your spouse, your mother—but it ultimately comes down to you. This book gives you a totally new way to think about your job. But the book won't do it for you. You must make the changes.

It's not difficult. As you read, think about the stories and fundamentals and relate them to your work.

Ask yourself: How am I doing on **knowing?** How am I doing on **deciding?** How am I doing on **assigning?** How am I doing on **influencing?** How am I doing on **coping?** Then take whatever steps are necessary to improve.

CONTENTS

INTRODUCTION

Regardless of what you do for a living, the joy of doing it well is the same. Whether you are sitting on the board of directors of a Fortune 100 company or waiting on tables in a neighborhood restaurant, there is a great deal of satisfaction to be had from doing the best you can do. It earns you the respect of your peers, those who report to you, and your bosses. It increases your chances of being listened to, appreciated, and being compensated accordingly. It enhances the chances of being noticed and being offered more responsibility. And in this uncertain world where people are being displaced, technology is taking over, and competition threatens to eat up any organization, doing your best, day after day after day, will give you an edge.

For the purposes of this book, doing your best is the very definition of success. It is measured by how competently you perform all parts of your job requirements and meet all of your objectives. This book can't tell you what your job requirements are. If you have a boss, that is between the two of you. This book will not tell you what your objectives should be, other than to suggest you have no more than four or five major ones at any one time. But, through examples, this book will show you how to achieve and hold on to success—whatever your job.

Work itself is so very broad in scope it may seem impossible to come up with an approach that would apply to everyone in every situation. And yet, it's very doable if you look closely at the five components of work and learn to master each and all of them.

Ironically, it was while on vacation in Wyoming, witnessing the operation of a very successful cattle ranch, that I was able to pinpoint what constituted a good day's work and break it down. I then took a look back at my own experience, and that of people I've known and worked with, and realized that everything we do can, in fact, be broken into five categories: **knowing, deciding, assigning, influencing,** and **coping.** The key to success, then, is doing each of them and doing them very well.

The individuals I've used as models of success in this book might surprise you. They run the gamut from a young waitress in Sheridan, Wyoming, to the exalted leader of an Antarctic expedition, from the director of a boy's summer camp to the CEO of a high-technology firm, from an esteemed artist to the coach of an Olympic gold medal team, from a tailor's assistant to a president of the United States. Yet, as disparate as these individuals might seem, they have in common a demonstrated level of performance in one or more aspects of their work that contain valuable lessons for the rest of us.

Let's start with **knowing.** Regardless of what you do, you have an obligation to know what you are doing. You must know the field you are in and your job requirements. If you work for an organization, you must know all about it, its suppliers, and its customers.

It should come as no surprise to you to learn that Norman Rockwell, the preeminent American illustrator, knew what he was doing. What you should take note of, however, is how he acquired his expertise. Even if you never pick up a paintbrush in your life, believe me, you have something to learn from the success of Norman Rockwell—just as you do from Rosa Parks, Herb Brooks, and Dwight Eisenhower, whom we'll learn more about in the chapter on **deciding.**

Rosa Parks, a tailor's assistant, made a single, simple decision that sparked the Civil Rights Movement in America. Herb Brooks, a hockey coach, made hundreds of small, but very important decisions that gave us one of the greatest victories in sports history. And General Dwight Eisenhower was charged with one of the most important decisions ever made in the free world. Each one of these people has something to teach us about making good decisions and doing a good day's work.

A major part of any job, paid or otherwise, is accepting and giving assignments. Regardless of what you do, you will be accepting assignments from your peers and bosses and giving assignments as well. My favorite example of **assigning** is the director of a summer camp I went to as a youth. Charged (assigned) with the care of 36 young boys for the better part of a summer, he used his mastery of assigning to assure that none of us got homesick while in his care.

The very nature of the camp director's work made him a man of influence in all of our young lives. Such is not the case with everyone, even though **influencing** is, in fact, a major component of success. We have all known people of influence. We have all been influenced by some of them. The key to success, however, is becoming one of them. For that, we look to the story of Rachel Carson, an unassuming young woman who dared go up against some of the most powerful corporations in the country, thereby making the world a better place for all of us.

And, finally, we come to **coping.** It may never have occurred to you, but the importance of learning to cope with things beyond your control is grossly underestimated. But no one and no thing is ever in complete and total control. You may have mastered all the other components of work, but if you can't cope with any deviations from the norm, you will not find success. Abraham Lincoln didn't become president to lead his country through the greatest war it would ever know. But, when he found himself in that position, he rose to the challenge and saved the nation. The Antarctic explorer Ernest Shackleton did not expect his ship to be trapped in the ice and crushed. But when it was, he created a new plan and eventually led every single member of his expedition to safety. These two individuals had mastered every other aspect of their job, but it was their ability to cope that set them apart. And so it can be with you.

This book offers a totally new way to think about your work. It should also help you understand that success isn't necessarily relegated to those who have more or do more. Most importantly, I hope it inspires you to take the steps necessary to satisfy your job requirements always—thus doing the best you can all day, every day. Then, not only will you gain success but you'll hold on to it as well.

A DAY AT THE RANCH

TWO STORIES SHOWCASING
THE FIVE PARTS OF ALL JOBS

J ust recently, my wife and I took a vacation in Wyoming and decided to visit a cattle ranch that was owned by the younger brother of a very good friend of mine. For a number of months I'd been working on a book about success and what it takes to do a job well. The book was going slowly, and I thought a day on the ranch might help clear my head.

The ranch was located in northeastern Wyoming, about 60 miles east of Sheridan. It was a long, beautiful drive through a part of the country covered with rolling hills. The sky seemed to go on forever. As we approached the ranch, we were met by a bunch of loud, friendly dogs of uncertain heritage that announced our coming with glee. We arrived just as Bill and his wife, Mollie, were finishing up their morning coffee. They were both in their mid-50s and bore the healthy glow that hard, satisfying work in the outdoors brings.

I am basically a city slicker. My domain was high technology, and I'd been in business all my life. I climbed up the corporate ladder, specializing in managing the people who worked for me and for others. After retiring I became a management consultant. I had few prolonged forays into the great outdoors since my days at summer camp, and I'd certainly never been to a working cattle ranch before. So, when Bill invited me to tag along on an inspection tour of the ranch, I jumped at the opportunity. It never occurred to me that I could learn about "success" at a cattle ranch in the middle of nowhere, but I was quickly educated.

MY DAY AT BILL AND MOLLIE'S RANCH IN WYOMING GAVE ME A CLEARER VISION OF THE FIVE COMPONENTS THAT MAKE UP ALL WORK FOR ALL PEOPLE: KNOWING, DECIDING, ASSIGNING, INFLUENCING, AND COPING.

As we bounced along the unpaved road in the front of his pick-up, I could see that the ranch was flourishing. Bill's truck was new. The ranch itself was kept up. There was no deferred maintenance—no repairs waiting to be done. Fences were fixed, gates were hung, and everything had a fresh coat of paint.

"We've got about 30,000 acres here," Bill told me, "and about 800 purebred Red Angus cattle."

Red Angus, I learned, were far better than their black counterparts. Bill told me his slogan was, "Easy to calve. Easy to handle. Easy to feed. Easy to eat."

I was impressed. I asked Bill if he had always been this successful.

"Hell, no," he said. "We spent 25 years raising crossbred Hereford and Black Angus for beef—slugging it out in a highly competitive business."

"How so?" I asked.

"Well, we ranchers have a tendency to do things the same way 'grandpa' did. Calves are born in February or March, when the weather is at its worst. Then, in the fall, we sell them to feed lots, where they're fattened for market. That was the custom in this region, and no one ever questioned it. It was quite a struggle, and we wanted to grow. But, to expand our operation and make gains from the economies of scale would have taken a lot of capital, which we didn't have and couldn't borrow. It looked like we were headed nowhere fast."

Ironically, success came from an unexpected quarter, one that was unplanned.

While their kids were growing up, Bill's wife, Mollie, had been reading about Red Angus cattle, which, like most breeds of American beef, originated in Scotland. The Angus breed was introduced into America in the 1870s, and it soon became very popular, though the choice had been to select for black cattle. Red cows, however, kept cropping up in the gene pool, and it wasn't long before people started to realize that they were actually superior to their black counterparts.

Once the kids were grown, Mollie bought four purebred Red Angus heifers and started to establish a herd. Eventually all their cattle were Red Angus. Bill and Mollie then moved from natural breeding to the more precise and controlled methods of artificial insemination and embryo transfer. They stopped selling beef on the hoof and started selling breeding stock—that is, raising the cattle from birth, then selling the bulls and heifers to other ranchers so they could expand or improve their own herds. Then, a few years ago, they decided to change the calving season from mid-winter to May and June.

That decision alone helped Bill and Mollie cut their operating costs substantially. There were fewer calf deaths, and they saved money on special winter feed and windbreak structures. "I can't for the life of me understand why we didn't think of that sooner," Bill said. "Elk, buffalo, deer, and antelope are all born in the spring for a reason—not in the severe snow and wind of winter."

Another decision helped tip the scales in their favor even more. Mollie and Bill started holding their own auctions at the ranch twice a year to sell not only their stock but that of co-operators from as far as away as Texas, as well.

As we headed back to the ranch for lunch I started thinking about Bill and Mollie's decisions to switch their herd from Hereford and Black Angus to Red Angus, from beef to breeding stock, from winter to spring calving, and to holding their own auctions. I doubted if they had fully anticipated what a huge change in their lives these four, seemingly simple decisions would make. I reflected on decisions and the art of deciding and realized that it has not been given the attention it deserves. Few are taught the importance of (or how to make) good decisions. Yet, decisions—and making the right ones—are the cornerstone of success in any endeavor.

The marketing director of a large corporation might make a single decision—contrary perhaps to conventional wisdom—but critical to the success of a new product. The general manager of a large distribution company might make a decision to let a popular sales manager go who is not performing up to par and is not taking any steps to improve his performance. An executive of a high technology company might decide to spend a large portion of his or her time finding, challenging, coaching, and promoting people who perform well, thereby ensuring the success of the organization.

Decisions come in all varieties. People in all walks of life make them every day. The most critical ones, the ones with the greatest impact, are generally made at the higher levels of an organization or made by the high-powered individual contributors. Nevertheless, poor decisions made at the lower levels in an organization can have time-consuming, expensive, even disastrous consequences. If you are a self-employed entrepreneur, good decision-making is critical to your survival.

Deciding—and deciding well—surely is one of the key elements of a good day's work.

Later in the morning I visited with Mollie and the two young women who help her keep track of each and every bull, heifer, and cow they own—noting genealogy, weight-change-over-time, and other facts that are significant in selecting the best heifers and bulls to continually improve the herd.

On this day, however, they were working on the upcoming spring auction. They were expecting about 250 people, which is a sizeable event under any circumstance. This one would last two days!

The first day would be devoted to cattle viewing, then lunch, followed by a symposium

with leaders in the industry, then a steak barbe
cue. The actual auction of 130 bulls and 75
heifers would take place the following day,
along with breakfast, lunch, and an Easter egg
hunt for the kids. All bases were being
covered.

Mollie and her crew were working on the
catalogue that included pertinent data for every
bull and heifer up for auction. It included pic-
tures, as well, not just of the cattle but of Mollie,
Bill, the rest of their family, and people from past
auctions. It listed phone numbers of everyone
involved, directions to the ranch, as well as lodg-
ing and car rental information for attendees.
They had made the whole event so inviting, I was
sorry I was going to have to miss it.

"How'd you figure this all out?" I asked.

"Well, I didn't learn it in school," Mollie
laughed. "I was an English major.

"Actually, we started small and learned as
we grew. And we had some pretty good teachers.
Bill's father was a rancher with immense curiosity about everything, and he forced Bill to
think. My mother was a statistician and gave

me great advice on gathering data on each member of the herd and using computers."

It is clear that Bill and Mollie know the field they're in. They know it because they're doing the work, and they take the time to learn what they don't know in this extremely complex business. Not only do they need to stay current on cattle genetics, grass management, marketing, and auctioneering, they have to keep track of a myriad of governmental regulations ranging from fertilizer application to income tax. They read, talk to others, and attend a few symposiums each year. They are active members of the Red Angus Association, the seat of all knowledge of the breed. "Knowing" what they're doing is another cornerstone of their success.

Most working people think they know what they're doing. But some of them do not. While they may know and do enough to get by, how many do what needs to be done well? How many mechanics, do you suppose, actually talk to the drivers of the vehicles they maintain to find out if there are any warnings of trouble on the horizon? How many compare notes with other mechanics? How many are expected to continue their schooling in mechanics after they're employed? To really know what they are doing, they probably need to learn more in order to tap into their best performance—to do a good day's work.

The point here is not to pick on mechanics, per se; I know some very good ones who do all of the above. I could be equally critical of people in management and supervisory positions who really don't manage well and aren't particularly interested in learning how.

The point is **knowing**—and constantly adding to what you know about your job—is every bit as important as deciding.

As it approached noon, I could smell lunch cooking long before the dinner bell sounded. My wife and I were just about the first ones into the dining room. On pretty short order, however, everyone else turned up at the table: Bill, Mollie, all of the ranch hands, office help and three other visitors. It was quite a production, one that I learned happens there every day of the week except Sunday. On this particular day the veterinarian, the blacksmith and one of Bill and Mollie's customers joined us.

As Bill passed the potatoes, he made a point of engaging the newcomers in conversation. "What's new?" he asked, and we all got an earful. The customer had some concerns that Bill and Mollie were able to address right away. The veterinarian gave us all an update on some of the problems in neighboring herds and some new vaccines that would soon be available. And the blacksmith was able to let Bill know what he'd done that day and when he should come back.

Bill then turned to each of the ranch hands and asked them how things were going. It became clear that everyone knew what he or she was responsible for doing in the time agreed upon. Everyone sitting at that table learned what had been happening on the ranch over the last 24 hours. Everyone had questions. Everyone received answers. Even I was starting to get the hang of this cattle ranching business.

Then it occurred to me that this was basically a staff meeting—each member giving his or her report; each one getting feedback from the boss and other members of the group. But it was one of the most effective and efficient meetings I'd ever sat through. Bill, who was already doing his job very well, was clearly on the lookout for ways to improve both his performance and that of everyone else.

He reviewed each of the ranch hands' current assignments. If expectations weren't being met, he found out why and asked what they planned to do to get back on schedule. Good performance was acknowledged with a "thank-you." Exceptional performance got a round of appreciative nods. And everyone left the table with a full understanding of what his or her next assignment was, including Bill. He needed to order some new tires for the flatbed truck.

I needed some time to think. I had just witnessed another component of top performance—**assigning**—and wanted to assimilate it.

Every member of the team had been given an assignment to carry out, had given an assignment to someone else, or had reported on an assignment. Some had done all three. Under Bill's guidance, they were all clearly adept at the process: setting objectives; communicating well with each other; holding others and being held accountable;

and giving and receiving consequences. I realized that assigning is a two-way street. The very act of giving an assignment incurs one—the follow-up—that is just as important as giving the assignment itself. The foreman who told Bill about the truck needing new tires will have to make sure that Bill does, in fact, order them—that's his assignment. Assigning and being assigned tasks was a major part of Bill's—and everyone else's—job, and Bill had clearly mastered it.

It turns out that this was going to be a particularly busy afternoon for Mollie and her crew; a busload of school kids was due to arrive at any moment for a field trip to the ranch. "Aren't you stretched just a little thin?" I asked. But Mollie just laughed and waved her hand down.

"You know what?" she said. "We always have time for friends and kids."

Bill and Mollie, it turned out, were just as involved in their community as they were in their work. They'd both been 4-H leaders and their living room was peppered with photos of kids with trophies and ribbons won at local fairs and livestock shows. Mollie taught Sunday school and Bill, I discovered, had served on the school board. These were people with influence—not just in their home and with their work at the ranch—but in the community as well. Couple that with their work with the Red Angus Association, and their influence extended nationwide.

It started me thinking: What is the value of success if it doesn't contain a component of influence? Through their influence, Bill and Mollie are able to touch the lives of people who've never met them and may never meet them. They have become role models. They own a 30,000-acre ranch and 800 head of cattle. They have successfully raised three kids and helped put them through college. They provide jobs for at least 10 people at any given time. But their real legacy just might be their influence.

I thought about whom I might have influenced in the course of my life and career, which then led me to think about who had influenced me. I realized even that was in my control and affected how well I performed. I chose whom I would believe, listen to, and follow. I chose whom I would question and dismiss. **Influencing** and choosing whom to be influenced by is probably the most overlooked and under-appreciated component of anyone's work. It often happens without either party being aware of its consequences, good or bad. It's the part of our work we must all pay very special attention to if we are to achieve a good day's work.

I was reminded of a woman I knew who worked as a first-level assembly operator in a small West Coast electronics plant. She had turned down numerous opportunities to become a supervisor because she knew she was in a place where she could do the most good for her community (recent immigrants who spoke little English). As an assembly operator, she would show new people around, and because she was multilingual, she could translate for them, encourage them to learn English, and recommend them to the employment office. Many people relied on her.

She was influential because she recognized their needs. It was the only way she could help people in her community find jobs at a good company that would treat them fairly.

Her influence came through helping other people, but influence can also come through knowledge, honesty, wisdom, determination, preparation and curiosity. It is an important component of a good day's work at every level.

While Mollie entertained the busload of kids that showed up, Bill and I had a few moments to ourselves. "This is a very well-run operation," I conceded. "How do you do it?"

"I have to confess," he said, "I did take one college course in business. And, believe it or not, I apply a few of the principles I learned there just about every day."

"Like what?"

"Well, first of all, I learned that I had to know and understand all the things for which I was responsible. So, if you were to put a fence around all of our acreage, I am responsible for the growth and well-being of everything inside the fence. That means I need to know everything that's going on inside the fence and, at the same time, be influential on certain matters outside the fence.

"The other thing I do is set four or five major objectives each year and hold myself responsible to meet them. My objectives for this year are to net $25,000 more than last year, to increase the sales from our auctions by 10 percent, to complete two new wells we are digging, and, as membership director of the Red Angus Association, to increase the membership by 12 percent."

I was clearly impressed with what looked like Bill's complete control over everything that happened at the ranch and told him so. He laughed.

"I wish," he said. "The weather is the real boss around here. Everything we do depends on it. There's either too much rain or not enough of it. It may be too cold in the winter and too hot in the summer. Either way, we have to deal with it. Then there's the issue of help. I happen to have a pretty good crew here right now, but it's hard getting 'em and keeping 'em this far from the city— no matter what we pay. There have been plenty of times we've had to make do with a lot less help than we needed.

"As much as I like to think I'm in charge around here, I'd be a fool if I believed it."

"Then how do you cope?" I asked.

"We remain optimistic. Blaming other people

and feeling sorry for ourselves is a luxury we can't afford. We hunker down and keep working, plugging along and figuring out ways to cope with whatever comes our way."

Until then I had overlooked the impact of things beyond our control on even the best day's work. Yet, that possibility looms large in everyone's endeavors. You can make all the right decisions, know your work inside out, make assignments with vigor, and have influence far and wide, but you also need to be able to cope with the unexpected. **Coping** wasn't a part of my thinking when I first went to Sheridan. But I added it before I left.

In all, my day at the ranch had been more successful than I ever imagined. It had cleared my head. I'd seen a good day's work in its purest sense and got a taste of success at a more visceral level than I'd ever been exposed to before. I had a handle on the five components that make up all work for all people: **knowing, deciding, assigning, influencing,** and **coping**. I felt I was on the right track; our next stop confirmed it.

✧

We arrived back in Sheridan in time to eat at the "best" restaurant in town, recommended by Bill and Mollie. They had spoken very highly about Julie, one of the waitresses, and she happened to be our waitress.

Julie, we had been told, was a single mom with two young children as well as an elderly mother and father to look after. Her husband had been killed in a freak farm accident five years before. At that time, with few other skills to fall back on, she had taken a job as a "hamburger joint" waitress. However, she had the talent and desire to be a waitress at the most expensive restaurant in town; so she moved up the waitress chain to the top spot where she makes a surprisingly good income.

WHEN I LOOKED AT JULIE'S PERFORMANCE AS A WAITRESS IN THE CONTEXT OF THE FIVE PARTS OF DOING A JOB WELL, IT WAS CLEAR THAT SHE KNEW HOW TO DO HER JOB EXTREMELY WELL.

Julie offered to take our coats and showed us to a table by the window, one of the best in the house. She gave us the menus and wine list, then told us about the dessert—a chocolate cake that sounded fantastic. Apparently it was going fast and she asked if we'd like her to set aside a couple of pieces for us.

On her way back to the kitchen she signaled one of the bus boys, who quickly brought us our water and a basket of warm bread and cold butter.

After a few minutes Julie came back to take our order. We discussed a few of the items on the menu, and she warned us off a couple of the more "innovative" dishes. Being in cattle country, we decided on a couple of steaks. I asked for mine "rare" and left it to Julie to do the rest. She had her assignment and hurried off to the kitchen to pass it along to the cook. Within moments we had our wine and salad.

It was a slow evening, and with this book in mind, I asked her who had influenced her the most as she learned to be a top waitress.

She said, "Everyone has been helpful. Partly, I suppose, because I asked them for help; and when I observed them doing something new, I asked them why. But the most help has come from the owner's wife. She has been my mentor and has pointed out what a top wait person does even if it is far from Park Avenue.

"Now I'm helping and giving suggestions to the new waiters and waitresses. The boss even has me interview most of the new job applicants. He told me that he liked my judgement."

My wife asked her how she coped with unpleasant, overly demanding customers.

She replied, "I tell myself each day as I drive to work that there will be two people today who will be totally unreasonable. So, when I get a blast from someone, I'm prepared. I just calm down, take some time, and sympathetically listen to them. If that doesn't lessen their emotions, I quietly tell them what I can do or what I can't do."

The entire meal went along flawlessly and the chocolate cake was, indeed, delicious. I couldn't help but look at Julie's performance in the context of the five parts of doing a job well. It was clear she knew how to do her job extremely well. She had made some excellent decisions—large and small—from taking this job to seating us by the window and suggesting the chocolate cake. She accepted the assignments she was given, assigned work to others where necessary, and was accountable throughout the meal. She certainly accepted help and influenced others. And it goes without saying that she was coping very well. Julie had taken her job as a waitress to its highest level. The consequence of Julie's exemplary performance was a pretty hefty tip, a clear mark of success in anyone's eyes.

Bill and Mollie successfully manage a ranch of 30,000 acres. Julie's domain is a restaurant that might seat as many as 40 people on a very good night. Yet, they have a lot in common. They are not captains of industry. None of them had ever received any formal training nor would they even consider that what they were doing has a logical rationale. Yet, in the simple act of going about their business in the best way they know how, they have achieved what we would all like to achieve: success.

Ask Yourself: Am I doing my job as well as Mollie, Bill, the assembly operator, and Julie are doing their jobs?

Keep them in mind as you go about your daily tasks.

KNOWING

THE TASK OF KNOWING YOUR JOB
THOROUGHLY

A n individual who is good at what he or she does is a wonder to behold. It does-n't matter if he or she is a virtuoso playing the violin or a stonemason building a seamless wall; there is nothing quite as inspiring as watching a master at work. I am just as much in awe of a politician working a crowd as I am of a schoolteacher captivating a classroom full of six-year-olds. They all fit my definition of success.

Knowing how to do a job well may come with experience. But that's not always the case. Julie, the waitress, actively learned how to do her job.

Mollie had never run a cattle auction before she staged her first, very successful one. Then there are a frightening number of people who've been at the same job for years and still aren't performing up to their potential.

Given that, there has to be more to doing a job well than simply doing it day after day after day—and there is. Some of the following fundamentionals might seem quite obvious. Yet, you'd be surprised at how often they are overlooked.

- **Put yourself in a position to excel.** Build on your strengths. If possible, take jobs at which you would be good, that you would like, and that you can do well. Then you'll be ready to go as far in job responsibility or job impact as your talent and desire will take you.

- **Know what is expected of you.** Others may think you already know. You may believe you already know. Don't make that assumption. Get a copy of your job requirements and refer to it often. If there isn't one, make one. Talk to people. Talk to the people you work for—your bosses and your customers or clients, both internal and external. And talk to the people who work for you. Find out what they expect of you. Help them do the best job they can do, and you will be helping yourself at the same time.

- **Know how to do the tasks involved in your objectives.** Like most people, you will have four or five major objectives that are to be met monthly, quarterly or yearly. Along with these you might have numerous small daily or weekly assignments (minor objectives). Be sure you know all about them and how to do them.

- **Be sure you fully know your job expertise.** If you are an accountant, know all the accounting needed for your specific job. If you are a firefighter, know all there is to know about fighting all kinds of fires.

- **Be constantly on the alert for ways to do your job better.** This may require a little extra schooling or reading or it might be as simple as paying close attention to a role model—someone whose work you admire. You might want to find a friend, mentor, or coach to help you, or you could form a network of people with relevant experience. Never pass up an opportunity to learn a little more. Take on new assignments that force you to stretch your mind. If no opportunities arise, make them.

- **Learn the field you are in.** Whether you're in entertainment, education or farming, you've got to know every aspect of that business, inside and out. Join professional organizations. Read books and magazines. Attend trade shows and conferences. Even if you've been in the field a long time, new developments in that or related fields should be keeping you on your toes.

- **If you're part of an organization, take the time to learn its structure and how it operates.** Be curious about how the people around you think and operate.

- **Learn the organization's culture—its values and its customs.** Don't assume that you are going to waltz onto the scene with the solution to everything that ails it. Show some respect for what has been accomplished to date. You may be bringing a wealth of experience or youthful enthusiasm with you, but every situation is different. Find out what the organization has tried and failed or succeeded at in the past. Find out about your organization's customers, suppliers and competitors. Understand the community in which you work. Keep your eyes and ears open. I can't say this enough.

FOR THE EXCEPTIONAL PERSON

If you are one of those "one out of 100" people whose talent and performance is so exceptional that you could break many of the rules and still be wanted and well paid—*don't*. Be on the team and make the team better. You'll be happier and everyone else will be happier and more productive.

These fundamentals aren't restricted to people in business; they apply to people in all walks of life, including the arts. Take Norman Rockwell, for example, the quintessential American illustrator. Over the course of nearly half a century, he produced more than 300 covers for *The Saturday Evening Post*, a weekly magazine. He is easily one of the most recognized American artists of the 20th century.

Rockwell was quoted in a 1923 issue of *International Studio*: "People somehow get out of your work just about what you put into it, and if you are interested in the characters that you draw, and understand them and love them, why, the person who sees your picture is bound to feel the same way."

Rockwell's work spanned most of the twentieth century—from asking young men to join the fight in the First World War to showing us astronauts landing on the moon in 1969. His paintings of the "four freedoms," inspired by Franklin D. Roosevelt's 1941 State of the Union address, raised $132 million in war bonds. Rockwell's paintings are among the most reproduced in history. In his later years, Rockwell had the freedom to create paintings that shared some of his deepest concerns—poverty and civil rights. Who can forget the image of little Ruby Bridges on her way to school—escorted by federal marshals? In 1976 Norman Rockwell received one of America's highest civilian honors, the Presidential Medal of Freedom.

Rockwell had the work of Winslow Homer, Frederic Remington, Charles Dana Gibson, A.B. Frost and Howard Pyle to inspire him as he was growing up. When he was 14, he started formal art training at the Chase School of Fine and Applied Art and left high school during his sophomore year to study art full-time at the National Academy of Design. He went on to study at the Art Students League in New York.

While there, one of Rockwell's teachers was Thomas Fogarty, who insisted his students "live" in their illustrations. They had to "know" the people they were painting, why they did what they did, where they lived, what the weather was like, and so on. One of Rockwell's great strengths was how he made us so familiar with the characters in his work. These are people we know—our friends, our family, our countrymen. We all remember Thanksgiving the way he depicted it—as if it was our Thanksgiving memory. His paintings had—and still have—the power to move us.

NORMAN ROCKWELL WAS BORN WITH A CERTAIN AMOUNT OF TALENT, BUT HIS ENDURING SUCCESS CAN BE ATTRIBUTED TO HOW HE DEVELOPED IT—HOW HE CAME TO KNOW AND UNDERSTAND WHAT HE WAS DOING.

Another of his teachers and mentors was George Bridgman. "You can't paint a house until it's built," he admonished his students. This was a lesson Rockwell took to heart. Just look at the hands of the characters in any Rockwell painting, and you can see how well he understood the underlying anatomy—the bone structure, the musculature—and the history of a life revealed in the texture of the skin.[1]

No doubt Rockwell was born with a certain amount of talent, but his enduring success can be attributed to how he developed it—how he came to know what he was doing. He had mentors in his teachers and in the masters whose work he studied assiduously: the elder Brueghel, Holbein, Ingres, Picasso and Rembrandt, whom Rockwell considered the greatest painter of all time.

Rockwell knew the business he was in and what was expected of him—images that grabbed our attention in just a few seconds, that were filled with people we recognized, and that depicted situations we understood. He fulfilled his job requirements and met his objectives.

He knew what he was doing. As a result, his work is as popular today as it was 50 years ago, and his success continues a quarter century after his death.

I recently had lunch with two young friends of mine, Joan and Mike, a married couple I have known for more than 20 years. Mike designs integrated circuits, and Joan is the president of a publicly traded company that manufactures integrated circuits. They both have master's degrees from Stanford University and together are raising two beautiful children, now 12 and 14. As the meal progressed I realized that Joan and Mike, in spite of the very different nature of their jobs, have mastered the "knowing" component of their work.

"My first job, 20 years ago, was as a circuit designer," Mike told me. "And that's what I am today. I am a staunch individual contributor. I always knew I wanted to play a role in the making of things like computers, television sets, telephones and other electronic gizmos, and that's exactly what I do." If the measure of Mike's success is how many of his designs sell, then he is very good at it.

Mike's circuit designs end up as silicon chips (integrated circuits) that are manufactured in a silicon wafer fabrication plant, electronically tested, then shipped to a plant where they are assembled into a plastic or ceramic jacket and offered for sale to the electronics industry. They are combined onto circuit boards with resistors, capacitors, connectors, power supplies and other

JOAN AND MIKE, A MARRIED COUPLE, FOLLOWED VERY DIFFERENT PATHS; YET BOTH MASTERED THE "KNOWING" COMPONENT OF THEIR WORK AND HAVE ACHIEVED THE PINNACLE OF SUCCESS BY DOING WHAT THEY DO VERY WELL.

components from other companies—to create, for example, a home computer.

To design a circuit that is going to be successful in the marketplace, Mike has to work with marketing people, application engineers and system designers who represent not just his clients, but their clients, as well. He has to stay on top of his field and every field that might have a use for his products. To do this he reads trade journals and magazines, takes courses, goes to industry trade shows and conferences, talks to other designers, buys and uses the end products, and stays alert. He also has to think ahead—to find a need and see what he can do to fill it. He has to work efficiently. The window of opportunity for the design-in-time of integrated circuits is about six to twelve months. If Mike can't meet that time frame, he has failed.

"I get a great deal of personal satisfaction from being the center of my very little world," he said. "If I could spend the rest of my working life continuing to design complex chips that sell like hot cakes, I would be a very happy man."

At that, Joan laughed. "Don't let him fool you. He's not sitting back in an easy chair, smoking a pipe with his feet up, contemplating his success. He puts in a full day, everyday, but about once a year he puts in a week or so of 14-hour days to meet a deadline. To stay exactly where he is—at the top of his game—he has to deliver top performance all of the time."

Joan, too, is at the top of her game, but she has her sights set on the next rung on the ladder. She also graduated from Stanford with a master's degree in electrical engineering and became a circuit designer, as Mike did. She enjoyed the work, but didn't love it. However, she was fascinated by the people side of the business: how the company was organized; how it was managed; and who was selected to do which jobs. After just a few years as a circuit designer, Joan enrolled in Santa Clara University's Leavey School of Business and got another master's degree. She then decided to apply what she had learned by getting a job as a first-level manufacturing supervisor in a company that made integrated circuits. Fourteen years later, she is the president of an integrated circuit manufacturing company that employs 500 people!

"Business school did not really teach me how to hands-on supervise or manage people," she confesses. "I learned that the same way everyone else does—on the job. And my first year was hell. The bosses demanded more output per day with faster throughput time from my crew, and they still expected fewer rejects per lot. My peers wanted their schedules met. The engineers had their special requests. The human resources people were driving me crazy. And the people who worked for me were full of excuses and constantly testing my competence and patience.

"Finally I just said, 'Hold it! Hold everything!' I sat down with my boss and told him how frustrated I was. He told me to ask the people who reported to me what they needed to do their jobs better and then provide it for them— which I did. I also took the job requirements I'd been given and rewrote them in language I understood. Then, after talking to the people on my shift, I made additions to the requirements. Once I understood what was expected of me, I could go out and learn what I didn't already know. Pretty soon I could do everything that was expected of me, and more. I not only learned how to do that job, I also learned how to go about learning to do any new job that I might take—and I've been applying that methodology ever since."

Once she'd mastered the manufacturing side of things, Joan moved on to marketing and sales and learned, first hand, how the organization functioned from those perspectives and how it functioned in the outside world. It was just a matter of time before she ascended to the presidency. "Now that I'm in the driver's seat," she says, "I have the final word on the company's direction, allocation of expenses, and human resources. Everyone else has some input, but I have the last word, and I'd better be right a lot more often than I'm wrong."

Learning how to learn new jobs isn't the only thing that got Joan where she is today. She also had intelligence and drive and ambition. By doing her job well and constantly looking for ways to improve her performance, Joan moved from supervisor to president in just 14 years, and she's not done yet. Her next step is to either build the company she's in or to tackle a much larger company.

In either case, Joan and Mike are both on the right track. They both started out in the same place, but with different professional goals and visions. They followed very different paths; yet both have achieved the pinnacle of success by doing what they do very well.

Ask Yourself: How am I doing on knowing?

From time to time, reread the fundamentals and take appropriate actions that let you do your best.

MANAGERS, TAKE NOTE!

Managers have an additional challenge. Not only must they meet their job description and objectives, they must design and put in place the structure of the organization (plans, practices, procedures, processes and rules).

■ Part of their responsibility includes making sure the organization itself is competent, that it has a clearly communicated vision, a well-thought-out strategy, and clearly stated and practiced values ("what we stand for around here").

■ There must be a sound organizational structure in place including: good planning; many ways to listen

---

and inform; sound human resource practices; good accounting and control procedures; a fair and competitive compensation plan; good meeting practices; sensible use of teams; good operating policies, practices, and procedures; and ingrained ways to continuously satisfy customers/clients, reduce defects/errors, lower costs, and do things faster.

■ Appropriate financial, human, and physical resources must be available for whatever assignments are made and then removed when no longer needed.

■ Look for and try to hire talented, capable, knowledgeable people for all positions and make appropriate training available for them to learn their jobs and continuously improve. Outside experts should be engaged when necessary.

■ A system for rewarding good performance and dealing with poor performance needs to be in place. Celebrate group achievements. In addition, there must be consequences to people's performance. Those who complete their assignments and meet their objectives should be appreciated appropriately—with thank yous, and/or gifts, bonuses, and promotions. Those who do not meet their objectives need to be reviewed and appropriately reprimanded, transferred, or asked to leave the organization. But these disciplinary actions should occur only after determining their poor performance was not because of circumstances beyond their control, and that they were helped as much as possible to meet their objectives.

■ Too often, in organizations striving for excellence, the human traits of the people are overlooked. Managers must be sure that all people have, as far as possible, good human traits. They should be cooperative and emotionally mature, articulate, enthusiastic, trustworthy, energetic, available to listen to others, persistent, self-confident, optimistic, curious, have a sense of humor, empathetic, patient, persuasive, helpful, demanding of good performance, and straight-forward ("they tell it like it is").

■ Managers should not interfere, but they should be willing to confront issues and end conflicts quickly. People in top management must strive for top performance if they expect those they work with to do the same. They should, above all, set a good example.

■ It is also managers' responsibility to make sure their people have good job requirements and objectives. Managers must help them meet their job requirements and attain their objectives.

Most importantly, an organization is only as competent as the sum of the individuals who make it up, with a preponderance of the impact coming from the high-income people.

---

[1] "Norman Rockwell, Artist and Illustrator," Thomas S. Buechner (Harry N. Abrams, Inc. 1970)

DECIDING

THE ART OF MAKING GOOD DECISIONS

Everyone makes decisions. Julie, the waitress, makes a multitude of decisions every day—so many, in fact, that a few poor ones might not have much impact on the cumulative effect of all the good decisions she makes. Bill and Mollie have similar, small, day-to-day decisions. The big ones—switching to Red Angus, switching to breeding stock, switching to spring calving, switching to auctioning their own stock—were huge and potentially very beneficial or very costly. They covered themselves by taking it one small step at a time. They started with four Red Angus and slowly built the herd to eight hundred. They did not, as they say, "bet the farm."

Mike is part of the decision process as to which integrated circuit to work on next, but every decision regarding its layout is up to him. His decisions might seem small compared to those made by his wife, Joan, the president of a high-tech corporation; but Mike could, very well, come up with a product that is a blockbuster. The quality of their decisions, just like the quality of Norman Rockwell's decisions for each stroke of his brush, were key to their success.

Good decision-making is essential to the success of any endeavor. Yet, many decisions, even important ones, are made with relatively little attention paid to their potential impact. Take the story of Rosa Parks, for example. When she left work on December 1, 1955, she had no idea that she was about to make a simple decision that would change the course of our nation's history.

Rosa Parks was a tailor's assistant, an African-American descended from slaves. After a long day's work, she boarded a bus in Montgomery, Alabama, and took a seat somewhere near the middle of the bus. But, at the next stop she was told to get up and move to the back of the bus to provide a seat for a white passenger. Rosa Parks simply refused. Her arrest led to the Montgomery bus boycott, which lasted almost a year. Her decision to appeal her conviction led to a Supreme Court ruling that made segregation against the law. In the eyes of many, Rosa Park's decision gave birth to the civil rights movement in the United States.

ROSA PARKS MADE A DECISION THAT CHANGED AMERICA'S HISTORY BECAUSE SHE KNEW SHE WAS DOING THE RIGHT THING. SHE ALSO POSSESSED A GREAT DEAL OF COURAGE.

Rosa Parks knew, deep inside, that she was doing the right thing. She knew the consequences and fully understood the alternatives. She also had a great deal of courage.

There's no way to guarantee that all of the decisions you make are going to be good ones. You can, however, significantly reduce the risk of making a bad one by heeding the following fundamentals:

- **Keep your eyes and ears open.** You should be constantly on the alert for problems and opportunities that beg for your decision-making skills.

- **Choose, with care, which decisions deserve your attention.** Focus first on the critical decisions that will have the greatest impact.

- **A condition postponed, avoided, or not considered is a decision.** Often, it is not a good decision. Look for problems and opportunities. Get your arms around them.

- **Gather all the facts.** Be curious. Talk to others and listen, really listen, to what they have to say. Get expert advice, if necessary, not just on the decision itself, but on how you're going to implement it. Get different points of view from different groups of people.

- **Collect questions to ask.** Because "the question that has not been asked cannot be answered," get questions from anyone who is knowledgeable about the subject.

- **Consider alternative choices.** Don't fall in love with the first idea. Be resourceful, creative, insightful, and imaginative. Listen to other people's ideas, then winnow the wheat from the chaff.

- **Understand the terms surrounding a decision.** The choice you make may have attendant terms and conditions. There may be fine print. There may be legal and ethical issues. Make sure you consider them all and their implications before making your decision.

- **Weigh the risks.** Compare them to the benefits. Think of all possible unintended consequences. Be sure you have the resources in place to successfully implement the decision. If two choices are very close, just pick one and proceed. If there's a risk involved, proceed with caution. If the risk is big, take a small bite or go slowly.

- **Pay attention to your inner thoughts and hunches as you go about your work.** There is a place for intuition.

- **Have courage.** Be sure you are constitutionally able and mentally prepared to see the decision through to its desired results.

- **Trust yourself.** Once you've made your decision, act on it. Don't dillydally—move forward as expeditiously as possible.

One of the most monumental, consequential decisions in history was made by General Dwight Eisenhower as Supreme Commander of the Allied

Forces during World War II—the launching of the
D-Day invasion of Europe on June 6, 1944.

The invasion was originally slated for
Monday, June 5th. Naval units began their
deployment on June 3rd. However, on June 4th,
COUNTLESS DECISIONS LED UP TO GENERAL DWIGHT D. EISENHOWER'S MONUMENTAL DECISION THAT CHANGED THE OUTCOME OF WORLD WAR II. the English Channel had its worst gale
in 20 years! Many of the ships and
landing craft were already on their
way to their rendezvous points, and
the men aboard the ships were badly
tossed about by the storm. When the
meteorologists determined that the
weather was clearing, Eisenhower asked for opinions. The response was mixed. It was up to him.

"I am quite positive we must give the order
to proceed as planned," he told those assembled
at his headquarters. "I don't like it. But there it is.
I don't see how we can do anything else."

The enormity of his decision can't be over-
stated. The lives of 3.5 million soldiers, sailors, and
airmen from Great Britain, the United States,
Canada, Australia, New Zealand, France, Belgium,
Norway, Poland, Czechoslovakia and the
Netherlands were on the line. Countless other

decisions—who, how, where, and when—had all led up to this one defining moment. Had Eisenhower not gathered all the facts, considered all the alternatives, weighed all the risks, or trusted himself to make the right decision, the outcome could have been very different.

Few, if any, of us will ever have to face a decision with such far-reaching implications. Nevertheless you should never discount the potential impact of every decision you make, no matter how seemingly insignificant.

Here's a case in point. When I was the general manager of Corning's Laboratory Products Division, our only product was Pyrex brand laboratory glassware. However, we had just started developing an electronic instrument with glass electrodes that could measure the quantities of sodium and potassium in liquids and the degree of acidity for liquids. Already on the market, and a large market at that, were instruments that measured the acidity of solutions—pH meters, and this market was served by one dominant supplier and 10 or so smaller suppliers.

A pH meter is a relatively simple, low-priced instrument—a glass-encased electrode attached to a cable that plugs into a meter. When the electrode is inserted into a solution, the meter registers the pH. However, the glass probes are subject to breakage, tend to get gunked up and need to be replaced often. So, in addition to the market for the meters, there was a good replacement market for the probes as well. The large instrument company decided to abandon the dealer network that we both used and started selling all of its products directly to its end customers.

This was not just an opportunity; it was a *good* opportunity. However, in our haste to get our new pH meter on the market, we came very close to blowing it with one simple, poor decision.

We wanted to get this product on the market as quickly as possible, so everyone in the development group turned their attention to it. To speed things up, our product development and production departments decided to use an off-the-shelf plug and receptacle. On the surface it looked like a good idea. But, as a result, the plug was not going to be compatible with the receptacle on most meters that were already on the market—the one produced by the large instrument company. Likewise, most of the electrodes that were already on the market—again produced by the large instrument company—would not plug into our meters. No one had stopped to weigh the consequences of this decision, with one exception—our marketing director. His intuition told him that this was a mistake. Our research eventually confirmed it.

AS GENERAL MANAGER OF CORNING'S LABORATORY PRODUCTS DIVISION, I LEARNED YOU CAN NEVER DISCOUNT THE POTENTIAL IMPACT OF EVERY DECISION YOU MAKE, NO MATTER HOW SEEMINGLY INSIGNIFICANT.

We started calling the dealers who would be selling the new pH meters to ask them if they thought the plug incompatibility was going to be an issue. One after another, they all said "No." After all, none of the electrodes made by the smaller manufacturers were compatible with those of the dominant manufacturer.

Then one of the dealers, the tenth one we talked to, said, "Are you crazy? You've got to change that plug! We want to sell electrodes that will fit the meters that are already out there. And, we want to sell meters that fit the replacement electrodes that our customers may have already bought."

Immediately, the marketing director called a meeting.

"How much would it cost to change the plug? And how long will it take?"

The extra cost, it turned out, would be negligible and the delay a mere two months. Without further ado, the changes were made.

A potential disaster had been averted and the sales and profits from the new pH meters exceeded everyone's expectations. Why? Because of good decision-making.

By being alert, considering the opportunities and weighing the risks, we were able to seize an opportunity to expand our business. By gathering all the facts, considering alternatives and having courage, the marketing director was able to turn a good opportunity into one that had significant positive consequences, not just for the company, but for himself, as well. It wasn't long before he became a vice president and division manager.

✧

Success rarely rests on a single decision, no matter how well it is made. There are four other parts of the equation to take into account: knowing, assigning, influencing, and coping. Not only that, most decisions are multifaceted and exponential in character. One decision (the decision to start making pH meters, for example) led to several others (whether or not to make them compatible with existing components, for one) that each led to several more. Each of the subsequent decisions must be considered with as much diligence as the first. This is true for small decisions as well as large decisions.

One of the most memorable moments in sports history—the remarkable defeat of the Soviet men's ice hockey team by the United States during the 1980 Olympic games in Lake Placid, New York— was as dependent on good decision-making as it was on athletic ability. The individual we have to thank for that moment is coach Herb Brooks.

I have more than a passing interest in ice hockey; my father-in-law, John Chase, was the captain of the 1932 U.S. Olympic team, which won a Silver Medal, also at Lake Placid.

No one in his right mind would have bet on the young U.S. team Brooks pulled together for the 1980 games. The Soviet Union had won five of the previous six Olympic gold medals and had dominated international "amateur" hockey for years. Its players were all in the Russian Army and played hockey 12 months a year. Brooks' team was composed of college and ex-college players, not professional athletes. Just a few weeks before the Olympics, the Soviets had routed the Americans 10-3 in an exhibition game at Madison Square Garden. Yet, in the semifinals at the Olympics, the U.S. team took a 4-3 lead against the Soviets with 10 minutes left to play. All they had to do then was to hold the Russians back, which they did. As the final seconds ticked away, an overwrought announcer exclaimed, "Do you believe in miracles?"

THE STORY OF HERB BROOKS AND AMERICA'S "MIRACLE ON ICE" IS ABOUT DECISIONS, ONE GOOD ONE AFTER ANOTHER.

He should have shouted, "Do you believe in decisions?"

The story of Herb Brooks and his winning team is about decisions—one good one after another—from his initial decision to coach the team to the decision to switch out his players every 35 to 40 seconds rather than up to 90 seconds for the Russians. The "miracle on ice" would not have happened had any of those decisions not been made correctly.

Brooks carefully considered every single player proposed for the team. Every one he accepted represented a significant decision on Brooks' part, as did every player he turned away. "I'm not looking for the best players," he told a colleague. "I'm looking for the right players."

Nor did Brooks let his personal feelings stand in the way of his main objective: to beat the Russians at all costs. His decisions were based on the facts. One of the best players in college hockey at the time was Mark Johnson, the son of legendary coach Bob Johnson—one of Brooks' bitter rivals. Putting Johnson on the team might have been a tough pill for Brooks to swallow, but putting him on the team was the *right* decision. It was Mark Johnson, the top scorer in college, who made the goal that tied the score with the Russians, clearing the way for Mike Eruzione's winning goal.

Once Brooks had chosen his team, he decided how to motivate them, how to play them, and how to rest them. Thinking goalie Jim Craig might need a little "inspiration," Brooks told him he might have made a mistake playing him so much. Any other player might have been devastated by a comment like that. But not Craig. It made him angry, angry enough to face the Russian onslaught with confidence. Brooks, constantly on the alert for problems and opportunities, wasn't above making everyone mad at him if it improved their chances of winning.

He gathered all the facts. Brooks not only studied every member of his team, he studied every player on the Soviet team, as well, until he knew their strengths and weaknesses as well as those of his own team. It paid off. He found their weak spots and took advantage of them.

When the Lake Placid game was over, Valery Vasiliev said, "After we were ahead at the end of the second period, we were already celebrating. Nobody can skate with us in the third period."[1]

But Brooks proved him wrong. His American team skated furiously in the last period, first to score the tying goal, then to score the go-ahead goal, and lastly to hold off the attacking Russians as time ran out. Brooks had forced his players into peak condition, and he had them work short shifts enabling them to always skate at top speed.

"Play your game. Play your game," Brooks kept telling his players as he paced behind them on the bench. He said the words from the side of his mouth. For all his demands on the players for all those months, he was a different person when he managed a game behind the bench, a thin-lipped general who exuded confidence and control and rarely lost his cool.[2]

As a result the Americans were able to keep the Russians at bay for 10 agonizing minutes. When the final buzzer sounded, the arena exploded. The results of that single moment, all those good decisions, continue to reverberate today.

Ironically, it was a bad decision that brought Brooks' brilliant career and life to a very sad end in the summer of 2003. He fell asleep at the wheel of his car on his way to the airport and was thrown from it as it rolled off the road. Sustaining fatal injuries, he died at the scene. Most agree the accident was survivable, had Brooks made the decision to wear his seatbelt that day.

Ask Yourself: How am I doing on deciding?

Analyze your past decisions—good and bad—to find the fundamentals on which you are weak. Then, take corrective action.

---

[1] "The Boys of Winter," by Wayne Coffey (Crown Publishers, New York, 2005)
[2] Ibid

ASSIGNING

THE DISCIPLINE OF ASSIGNING AND
BEING ASSIGNED TASKS

Assigning involves much more than simply asking someone to do something. It involves accepting assignments as well as giving them. It includes making sure that everything is in place to get the job done. It includes regular, periodic follow-up. It occurs at all levels of the organization, and assignments can be passed both vertically (up and down the level of responsibility) and horizontally (peer to peer). And it definitely includes assigning tasks to yourself.

Remember the noontime meal at the ranch? Bill doled out plenty of assignments, but not without knowing that everyone receiving one was competent to do the job and had the time, equipment and material necessary. He even accepted an assignment from one of his ranchhands. There was a good feeling around the table, which created a willingness to get the job done. Everyone was fair, friendly, polite, enthusiastic and cooperative. They had good human traits.

Remember Julie, our waitress? She had an assignment from her boss about when she was expected to be at work and what she was expected to do there. She received an assignment from us (our order), then proceeded to see that it was carried out by everyone who needed to help her make our experience as enjoyable as possible. Her employer's job was to make sure she had all the tools she needed (a reliable cook and sufficient support staff) to carry out her job to our satisfaction. It was our responsibility to make sure she had all the information necessary to deliver our dinner in the manner in which we expected it. After delivering our meal, she stopped by to make sure everything was to our satisfaction.

Don't assume that because you ask someone else—even the boss—to do something, that it is going to get done. At the ranch, Bill accepted the responsibility for getting new tires for the truck, but the foreman needed to make sure Bill actually did it, without being a pest. Likewise, Bill has to make sure that the ranch hands feel comfortable checking up on the boss—a sign of real leadership. Doubtless, the new tires—or lack thereof—will come up at their next meeting.

Assigning has different implications and ramifications depending on whether you're the top person in the company, an individual contributor or a self-employed mechanic in a garage. It also depends on whether you are making the assignment or accepting the assignment. Regardless, the seven fundamentals of the art of assigning are the same. Master them all, and you will be well on your way to doing a good day's work.

- **Be competent.** Whether you are assigning work or being assigned a task, know what you are talking about. If you are accepting a job, make sure you can do it—that you have the time, the needed support from others, and the appropriate facilities, equipment, tools, and materials. If you are assigning a job, make sure all these things are in place for the assignee. This may require thoughtful planning or just plain common sense. In other words, don't go into a steak house in the middle of Wyoming and demand a serving of quiche.

- **Be fair, friendly, polite, cooperative and ethical.** Have good human traits. Nobody gets inspired by or wants to work with someone who is a grouch or can't be trusted. Herb Brooks was not a pleasure to play for, but the players on his team respected and trusted him.

- **Make sure your objectives are well defined and clearly understood by the person accepting the assignment.** Before the work starts, both parties must agree upon objectives that are SMART: Specific, Measurable, Agreed-upon, Realistic and Time-bound (that is, they have an agreed-upon completion date). Discuss the assignment fully and listen to the assignee's point of view.

- **Communicate with all concerned.** On assignments of some magnitude, tell everyone who might be impacted by the assignment what to expect. Of equal importance is to listen—listen to other's ideas, suggestions, opinions, and concerns.

■ **Do the assignment**. Whether you have accepted an assignment from someone else or yourself, do it, and do it well. Work diligently, efficiently and effectively. Follow the instructions and don't take short cuts. Take a few minutes each day to do a personal system check. Did I do everything correctly? Did I do everything I should have done? Did I do everything I said I would do? Correct what went off course and look for ways to improve wherever possible.

■ **Hold yourself and others accountable.** Making an assignment garners an assignment. Don't ever assume it's being taken care of. Follow through. At the same time, make sure you're doing your part to ensure your goal is achieved. Does the assignee have the tools and time he or she needs? Is the agreed-upon objective clear? If it's not, find out what you need to do to make sure it is. Set new deadlines and/or modify the objective. By helping others improve their performance, you improve yours as well.

■ **Make sure there are consequences.** Those who complete their assignments and meet their objectives should certainly be appreciated and those who don't should be reprimanded (see Managers, Take Note! in Chapter Two).

The key to mastering the art of assigning is to do all parts well. If a single part is left out or done poorly, all could be for naught. They all apply whether the task is as simple as ordering dinner in a restaurant or making a major change in a large organization. And the larger and more complex a change—for example, the making of a slow-moving organization into a nimble, fast-moving organization—the more critical it is to do each part extremely well.

One of the finest examples of assigning I've ever experienced occurred at a summer camp I attended many years ago. I was one of 36 young boys to attend this particular camp, which was eight weeks long—a very long time. It was back when a long-distance telephone call cost nearly a day's wages. Consequently, the camp director decided that we would all write a letter home two times every week. That was his goal: 16 letters per boy, 576 letters in all.

The letter-writing task was announced at our first camp meeting. The director made it clear that a letter home would be due from each of us, by suppertime, every Wednesday and Sunday—no exceptions. The assignment was clear and concise. His objective was well defined and clearly understood. In other words SMART: Specific, Measurable, Agreed-upon, Realistic, and Time-bound.

He also reminded us every Wednesday and Sunday at lunch. During the hour-long rest period in our cabins that followed, our two counselors not only reminded us, again, to write home, but they also encouraged

> **THE KEY TO MASTERING THE ART OF ASSIGNING IS TO DO ALL PARTS OF ASSIGNING WELL. ONE OF THE FINEST EXAMPLES OF ASSIGNING I EVER EXPERIENCED OCCURRED AT A SUMMER CAMP I ATTENDED MANY YEARS AGO.**

and helped us and thanked us when we were finished. The camp "store," open on Wednesdays and Sundays after lunch, was stocked with plenty of paper, envelopes, pencils and stamps, in addition to candy, toothbrushes, toothpaste and postcards. There was no question that the expectation was reasonable, that we were all competent to carry it out, and that we had all the tools necessary With very few exceptions, the letters were all completed and turned in during the time allotted.

At dinnertime, we would all gather together again in the cramped dining room where the boys from each cabin, and their counselors, sat at the table assigned to them. There were a total of six tables.

Before the general announcements, the director would ask, "Cabin One? All letters in?"

"Yes, *sir*," would be the head cabin counselor's reply.

"Cabin Two?"

"All letters in, sir."

"Cabin Three?" And so on, until every cabin had reported.

More often than not, the response was affirmative. Occasionally, however, the counselor might have to report "No," because the boy in question was usually in the infirmary or away from camp. The director then asked for, and was given, a day and time by which the missing letter would be turned in. He was holding himself and all of us accountable.

At the end of the report he thanked us all, but this wasn't the only "reward" we received. Not a week went by that each and every boy at that camp didn't receive at least two letters from home. Homesickness was rarely an issue, and letter writing became a habit.

The camp director, who was an educator during the winter, probably couldn't have made a list of all the parts of assigning if you gave him a month of Sundays. But, he had quite naturally and unwittingly made the task a practice that everyone followed 100 percent of the time. We're not all this fortunate, so we need to consciously think about and apply the seven fundamentals in order to master the art of assigning.

The consequences component of assigning is shown in one of my favorite stories. Andrew Carnegie, a poverty-stricken Scot who came to this country earning two cents an hour, eventually amassed a fortune so huge that he ended up giving $365 million of it away! He attributed his huge success to his ability to find out what the other person wants, and money, he discovered, even in modest amounts, is what often gets people's attention.

It turns out his sister-in-law was worried sick about her two sons who were students at Yale. They were so busy with their own affairs they couldn't find time to write home. Week after week she'd write, imploring them to respond. Week after week her letters went unanswered. Finally, Carnegie wagered a hundred dollars with one of his colleagues that he could get his nephews to write back to him, by return mail, without even asking them. Andrew Carnegie, of course, wouldn't have a wagered a hundred dollars without a foolproof plan, and he had one. He wrote the boys a nice, long, chatty letter and closed by mentioning that he was enclosing a five-dollar bill for each of them.

THE CONSEQUENCES COMPONENT OF ASSIGNING IS SHOWN BEST BY ANDREW CARNEGIE, A POVERTY-STRICKEN SCOT WHO CAME TO AMERICA, EARNED TWO CENTS AN HOUR, AND EVENTUALLY GAVE AWAY $365 MILLION OF HIS AMASSED FORTUNE!

He neglected, however, to enclose the money.

Sure enough, he heard back from them in no time. "Dear Uncle Andrew," they wrote. "Thank you for your very kind note. However…"[1]

Carnegie had found a way to get the boys to do what they should have been doing all along. Herb Brooks had to find another way to do the same for the American hockey team. He had been talking until he was blue in the face to get his guys to start playing like a team. The "Brookisms" have become the stuff of legends: "The name on the front of the jersey means more than the name on the back," he would tell them, referring to the name of the team versus the name of the player. But, it wasn't until he brought in outsiders, who might replace some of them just weeks before the Olympics, that they really started thinking and acting as a team, if only to keep the new guys out.

There are many notable examples in history of good assigning and decision-making, but none so compelling, perhaps, as that of the polar explorer, Sir Ernest Shackleton. By 1914, the North Pole had been reached by an American and the South Pole by a Norwegian. The last great prize to be had would be a trans-Antarctic crossing, a trip of more than 1,800 miles in sub-zero temperatures, blowing snow and freezing wind. Ernest Shackleton, who had led an earlier British expedition and been on another in search of the South Pole, decided that this prize would be his. On August 8, 1914, his ship, the *Endurance*, set sail from Plymouth, England. Headed for the Weddell Sea with 27 men and 56 sled dogs, this was an adventure of the highest magnitude. There would be no communication with the outside world except listening to an occasional wireless broadcast. The nautical instruments at their disposal would be a few incomplete maps, lead weights to determine the sea's depth, timepieces, binoculars, a sextant to tell them their location and an aneroid barometer to forecast changes in the weather.

Shackleton's objective was to cross, through the South Pole, from one side of Antarctica to the other, gathering scientific data along the way. It never happened. The *Endurance* never even reached the polar ice cap. Instead, the 144-foot ship became trapped in the ice of the Weddell Sea. Here, Shackleton and his men lingered for almost 300 days under abominable conditions, hoping to break free when the ice thawed. But before that could happen, the force of the shifting ice crushed the *Endurance* and she sank. Even so, Ernest Shackleton is considered one of the most successful leaders in modern history, and the outcome of this expedition offers a classic example of success.

As they abandoned the ship, Sir Ernest wrote later, "The task now was to secure the safety of the party, and to that I must bend my energies and mental power and apply every bit of knowledge that experience of the Antarctic had given me. The task was likely to be long and strenuous, and an ordered mind and a clear program were essential if we were to come though without loss of life. A man must shape himself to a new mark directly the old one goes to ground."[2]

SIR ERNEST SHACKLETON'S 1914 TRANS-ANTARCTIC EXPEDITION OFFERS A CLASSIC EXAMPLE OF HOW SUCCESS TRIUMPHED OVER TRAGEDY BECAUSE OF HIS ABILITY TO GIVE AND ACCEPT ASSIGNMENTS.

Shackleton and his men were now camped on an ice flow. Weeks went by and food became scarce. Their chances of survival looked worse and worse. So, when the ice drifted within a reasonable distance, they destroyed the last of their dogs and set out in three small, 20-foot lifeboats for a three-day sail to Elephant Island. Once there, Shackleton and five of his men took one of the boats on a treacherous, 16-day trip through the open ocean. Their destination was the whaling station at Stromness on South Georgia Island, 800 miles away, where they could get help. However, a freezing gale forced them to land on the other side of Georgia Island at King Haakon Bay. Frozen and bone-cold, they were still miles away from Stromness.

Shackleton had clearly been faced with an enormous number of decisions during this ordeal. None was as significant, perhaps, as the one he had to make next. The choice was to try to reach the whaling station by sea, another 150 miles in the open boat, or to cross the 4,000-foot-high ridge of mountains that separated him and his men from the whaling station, a mere 17 miles away as the crow flies.

He chose the latter and took two men with him over the glacier-clad mountains to find help. Lacking appropriate gear, they made do with what they had.

"I was unfortunate as regarded footgear," he later wrote, "since I had given away my heavy

Burberry boots on the floe, and had now a comparatively light pair in poor condition. The carpenter assisted me by putting several screws in the sole of each boot with the object of providing a grip on the ice. The screws came out of their lifeboat, the *James Caird*."[3]

Thirty-six painful, frozen, sleepless hours later, they reached Stromness. Immediately they found a ship that would take them around the island to pick up the three who had stayed with the lifeboat. However, it took almost four months and four trips by four different vessels to rescue the 22 men left behind on Elephant Island. Not a single one of his men perished throughout this horrific ordeal. By all marks, this was a successful endeavor, indeed.

Although Shackleton made many right decisions on this expedition, he made one very big, very bad decision. He had been warned by the whalers at South Georgia Island that this was one of the worst "summers" they'd ever seen in regard to the ice packs in the sea. Even so, Shackleton sailed the *Endurance* into the ice fields, and that is where the rest of the story unfolds. His ultimate success—getting all his men home alive—can be directly attributed to all the other things he did well, most notably, assigning.

Shackleton had personally interviewed and carefully chosen each and every member of the expedition. With the exception of one, they all had extensive cold-weather, sea-faring experience and knew what they were doing and what to expect. In addition to their standard daily chores, each also had a specialty crucial to the success of the original mission. For example, there were among his crew a ship's captain, a first mate, a cook, a photographer, two doctors, two scientific specialists, a carpenter and a navigator. The men were all of good temperament and treated each other with respect, except, occasionally, when under the most intolerable conditions.

Shackleton had received his training in the British Maritime Service and not the Royal Navy, where strict "command and control" caused a great deal of resentment between officers and crew. Maritime officers, however, basically trusted their crews and treated them as they would like to be treated themselves.

Shackleton did as much as he could to keep morale up, celebrating holidays and birthdays, organizing football games and dog sled races on the ice floe. When conditions worsened and they had to institute rationing, everyone—crew and officers alike—were treated equally. He listened closely to his key people. Nobody was left in the dark when he decided what course of action to take. As a result, Shackleton's men admired and respected him.

His assignments were clear and concise, and none was made without first considering all the facts. He looked at all the charts, considered the weather, obtained the latest bearings and sent someone ahead to reconnoiter when possible. His experience weighed heavily, as did his intuition. Accountability was rarely an issue—the very nature of their work and close proximity almost guaranteed it. His crew's motivation, of course, was significant; their very survival depended on it. Yet Shackleton never assumed that would be enough. His ability to give and accept assignments contributed significantly to their ultimate success.

Ask Yourself: How am I doing on assigning?

Assure yourself that you are competently using each of the seven fundamentals of assigning on every assignment, whether made by you or assigned to you.

Read history, find examples, and talk to others about how well or how poorly the fundamentals of assigning are conceived and carried out by you.

[1] Dale Carnegie, "How to Win Friends & Influence People" (New York: Simon & Schuster Inc. 1982).
[2] Sir Ernest Shackleton, South: the *Endurance* Expedition (New York: New American Library, 1999).
[3] Ibid

INFLUENCING

THE IMPORTANCE OF INFLUENCING
AND BEING INFLUENCED

Y ou may be the greatest decision-maker on the planet. You may do your job so well that people wait in line for hours on end just to see you perform. You may know how to get people to do your bidding at the bat of an eye. But, none of this contributes to a real good day's work unless you also have influence. And of equal importance is: Do you accept the influence of others?

Shackleton had an amazing influence on those under his command, and he acquired it quite simply. He did his job well and accepted all the hardships equally with his men. He never wavered or quit. He earned their respect. On returning home, he shared his experience through books and lectures and, as a result, became an inspiration to future explorers and even modern business leaders.

Herb Brooks' spirit continues to live in the heart of every player, every coach, and every spectator who knows his story—not only because of his Olympic victory, but also because of what he did afterward. He shared his passion and insight and devoted much of his life to improving the game of ice hockey both nationally and internationally.

IT'S NEVER TOO LATE TO LEARN FROM DALE CARNEGIE, A GRAND MASTER OF HOW TO USE YOUR INFLUENCE TO IMPROVE YOUR OVERALL JOB PERFORMANCE.

A common mistake is to assume that you do not have influence. Perhaps you are new to the job or relatively low on the totem pole. The fact is, however, that given careful consideration, everyone can be of influence and can use that influence to improve his or her overall performance.

A grand master of this was Dale Carnegie. His book, "How to Win Friends & Influence People," first published in 1937, has since sold more than 15 million copies.[1] That in itself is a lot of influence.

Carnegie's book should be basic reading for every high school graduate in the nation.

It is packed with advice and examples—all of them good but none so crucial as mastering the first step in the art of influencing—getting people to like you. Here are some quick tips culled from his book:

- You can make more friends in two months by becoming interested in other people than you can in two years by trying to get other people interested in you. Talk about the things he or she treasures most. Always make the other person feel important.

- Actions speak louder than words and none is more important than a smile. It says, "I like you. You make me happy. I am glad to see you."

- The average person is more interested in his or her own name than all the other names on earth. Remember it and use it often. You have paid a subtle and very effective compliment.

- Be a good listener. Listen with your ears and your heart. Exclusive attention to the person who is speaking to you is very important. Nothing else is as flattering as that.

The temptation is to assume that being a person of influence means becoming the great sage and offering advice whether or not it's requested. In "East of Eden," the Nobel Prize-winning author John Steinbeck wrote, "I guess the last bad habit a man will give up is advising."[2] I'm as guilty of that as anyone or I wouldn't be writing this book! But don't think for a moment that giving advice is the same thing as having influence. Influencing involves much, much more. It might even be a very large part of your job if you're in a staff position or in a situation where all else seems equal and the only tie breaker may be influence. Or it could simply be an artifact of your success.

In any case, mastering the fundamentals of influencing and accepting influence requires that you do the following:

- **Share your special knowledge.** No matter who you are or what you do, you have special knowledge—observations or insights about what you see happening around you that nobody else might have. It's your job to share this with others at appropriate moments.

■ **Choose your words carefully.** Make sure you're perceived as helpful rather than critical. "There's another way to do that," will get a better response than, "You're doing it all wrong." If it doesn't, the trick is to be persistent, but not annoying, and always remember that unsolicited advice is usually unwanted and resented.

■ **Have an open door and a listening ear.** The taller the bamboo, the lower it bends. Be open to new ideas, new directions, and new ways to do things. Don't bark at people or interrupt them. Don't tell them "we've already tried that" or "that idea is foolish." Don't shut them down if they're not articulate. Be someone people aren't afraid to approach; they might have something to offer that could very well improve your performance and reputation. They may not have a solution for the problem at hand, but they may be telling you about a different problem that needs to be fixed. Often people present information as a solution. "You ought to…," they might say. They may be wrong, but listen carefully anyway because they are telling you of a problem that begs your attention.

- **Help, teach, mentor or coach.** When asked, take the time to help others improve their performance. Your influence will grow by leaps and bounds. The difference between a person who is great and one who is simply famous is how much he or she helps other people.

- **You are on stage at all times.** Your influence spreads, positively or negatively, by what you say and how you act.

- **Be wary of those whose influence you accept.** Influence is a powerful tool. Despots throughout history have mastered its use to wreak havoc on the world. If you find yourself being influenced by others, make sure that they are a *good* influence.

- **Use the power of your position very judiciously.** The term "influence" implies that opinions are changed and tasks are started through reason and persuasion. It also implies that how well or how poorly tasks are done delivers rewards or pain. The term "power" implies that opinions are changed and tasks are started through threats of pain and promises of benefits not necessarily tied to performance. Power is a method that sometimes is necessary, but it should be used carefully and seldom.

Influence takes all forms—from the individual willing to serve as a mentor to the corporate executive who serves on a school board, an industry committee or a nonprofit board; from people who are elegant in the simple chores of daily life to individuals who have changed the course of history.

For people who hold staff positions within an organization, using the influence that goes with the position is often a major factor in that person's success and is often the key to the success of the organization as well. I am reminded of a chief financial officer with whom I once had the pleasure of working. He was never seen without his notepad, which consisted of the unused sides of used 8½-inch x 11-inch paper, stacked together on a clipboard. Although he urged spending when it was beneficial, there was no question as to how much value he placed on thrift, and that value trickled throughout the organization. When it came to helping managers control spending, he was one of the most influential people I have ever known.

Being of influence spans all types of individuals in all walks of life: from accountants to coaches, from teachers to politicians. By all counts, one of the most influential people of the past century was a shy, unassuming scientist and writer who took on—and prevailed over—the U.S. government and some of the largest corporations in the United States. Her name was Rachel Carson. In 1962, when the environmental movement was little more than a slogan ("Please, please, don't be a litter bug") and the United States was the greatest agricultural producer ever, she shocked the world with her book, "Silent Spring."

Carson grew up in the rural town of Springdale, Pennsylvania. She graduated from Chatham College in 1929 and received a master's degree in zoology from Johns Hopkins University three years later. She supported herself through the Depression writing radio scripts for the U.S. Bureau of Fisheries and feature articles on natural history for the Baltimore Sun. In 1937 she embarked on a career as a scientist and editor for the U.S. Fish and Wildlife Service. She shared her love for the beauty of the natural world by writing articles and books extolling its virtues, including a prize-winning study of the ocean called "The Sea Around Us", published in 1952. She retired from government service that same year to devote herself to writing.

As early as 1945, Carson became alarmed by chemical pesticide programs that were broadcasting poisons such as DDT throughout the environment. However, the potential hazards posed by DDT soon paled in her eyes compared to a new barrage of insecticides on the horizon—dieldrin,

FORTY YEARS AFTER SHE DIED, RACHEL CARSON CONTINUES TO INSPIRE AND INFLUENCE NEW GENERATIONS TO PROTECT THE LIVING WORLD AND ALL ITS CREATURES.

parathion, heptachlor, and malathion. Armed with knowledge, she reluctantly stepped outside her zone of comfort to warn the public about the long-term effects of pesticides.

Based on her observations of our use and abuse of chemical pesticides, "Silent Spring" predicted dire consequences for our future—a future devoid of songbirds that announce spring. She reminded us that we are just as vulnerable as all the other living creatures on the earth and that we must stop the destruction of our planet.

Carson was attacked by the chemical industry and assailed by threats of lawsuits. She was accused of being an alarmist, and it was suggested she wasn't qualified to write such a book. However, she had earned the right to challenge the use of chemical pesticides promulgated by agricultural scientists and her former employer, the U.S. government, and absolutely felt an obligation to do so. She used the strength of her research, the support of leading scientists and conservation organizations, and the courage of her convictions to back her up.

"Silent Spring" became a runaway best seller and was read the world over. In 1963, Carson was asked to testify before Congress, and she used the opportunity to call for new policies to protect human health and the environment. Though she died of cancer the following year, her influence is felt to this day.

Carson lived simply and celebrated the natural world she was trying to save, setting an example for all who would follow. She was confident about her facts as well as her ability to present them. She subjected herself to scorn, and even ridicule, yet remained calm in the face of her accusers. Because her research backed her up, she maintained the approval of her peers.

Forty years after she died, Rachel Carson continues to inspire new generations to protect the living world and all its creatures. She was not a born crusader, but an intelligent and dedicated woman who simply rose heroically to an occasion and used her influence to change the world.

Ask Yourself: How am I doing on influencing?

Read newspapers, obituaries, history, novels; watch movies; observe people influencing and being influenced.

Find role models in your organization and in your community to emulate. Help others.

---

[1] Dale Carnegie, "How to Win Friends & Influence People" (New York: Simon & Schuster Inc., 1982).

[2] John Steinbeck, "East of Eden" (New York: Penguin Books USA Inc., 1992).

COPING

THE NECESSITY OF COPING WITH
THINGS BEYOND YOUR CONTROL

What a wonderful world it would be if things always went the way we planned: if people were always understanding and agreeable; if the weather never misbehaved; and if we didn't have to deal with change. We could succeed with knowing, deciding, assigning and influencing. But that's not the world we live in. People can be ornery. The weather is still somewhat unpredictable and fickle. And constant change is a permanent feature in our lives.

Change is difficult for us. We like our coffee a certain way. We park our car in a certain place.

Our workspace is set up in a certain way and if someone comes along and changes things, we get mighty upset. So it is no wonder that when major changes come into our work (and they seem to be coming with more and more frequency), it doesn't tend to go down well with us.

That brings us to the last component of a good day's work, which we must master if we are to be a success. That component is coping—the task of working around and living with problems and issues that are beyond our power to control. With that—the final piece of the puzzle in place— success is well within reach.

Shackleton had to cope with the weather and every challenge it posed to his survival and that of his crew, both on and off the ice floe. He had to cope with diminishing food supplies and diminishing morale among his men. He had to cope with hunger, cold, and physical pain. But, he never gave in, and he never gave up. Had he not been able to cope, he and his men would not have survived.

It might serve you well to acknowledge that as bad as things may seem, they could be a whole lot worse. These words from Sir Ernest

Shackleton, describing the condition of the men left behind on Elephant Island for almost four months while he went to find a rescue ship, might help you put things in proper perspective:

The semi-starvation during the drift on the ice floe, added to the exposure in the boats, and the inclemencies of the weather encountered after our landing on Elephant Island, had left its mark on a good many of them. Rickenson, who bore up gamely to the last, collapsed from heart failure. Blackborrow and Hudson could not move. All were frostbitten in varying degrees; and their clothes, which had been worn continuously for six months, were much the worse for wear. The blizzard which sprang up the day we landed at Cape Wild lasted for a fortnight, often blowing at the rate of seventy to ninety miles an hour, and occasionally reaching even higher figures. The tents which had lasted so well and endured so much were torn to ribbons, with the exception of the square tent occupied by Hurley, James, and Hudson. Sleeping bags and clothes were wringing wet, and the physical discomforts were tending to produce acute mental depression. The two remaining boats had been turned upside down with one gunwale resting on the snow, and the other raised about two feet on rocks and cases, and under these the sailors and some of the scientists, with the two invalids, Rickenson and Blackborrow, found head cover at least.[1]

Bill, the cattle rancher, also has to cope with the weather, which he does by digging wells and building windbreaks. From time to time he has to cope with marginal ranch hands. And sometimes, when there simply aren't enough people to get the necessary work done, he has to cope with the overload. His business depends on his ability to cope.

Julie, our waitress in Sheridan and a single mother, has to cope with her two children, her aging parents, and, occasionally, with an unpleasant customer. The quality of her life depends on her ability to cope.

Rachel Carson had to cope with the hostility her predictions elicited. Yet, because she did, we all have a safer environment in which to live.

And Rosa Parks had to cope with being arrested, thrown in jail and convicted of breaking an unjust law. But, by doing so, she helped effect a change for the better for millions of people.

We have to cope with plenty of things in our lives. Customers can be difficult and unreasonably demanding. Bosses and peers can be rude, sloppy, lazy, prejudiced, weak, biased, unfeeling and…need I go on? Certainly, there are those who simply don't think you or what you have to say is all that important.

Suppliers may let you down. Customers may stretch their payments to you. Competitors may cut their prices. Your good boss may be replaced by a bad boss. And some of your people may leave you for better jobs, more money, or both. Your home situation, romantic situation and financial situation may leave a lot to be desired. And someone might steal your car!

It is how well you cope with these unexpected bumps in the road that distinguishes you from the rest. It is the true mark of success.

There are several fundamentals you should use to cope with things that happen beyond your control—to cope successfully with change and to ensure that, in spite of everything else, you can still put in a good day's work.

- **Accept that certain situations are beyond your control, and you simply have to deal with them.** Don't let anger or frustration get in the way of dealing with the situation at hand. Don't resign yourself to your fate, and don't start to question your own worth. Develop some toughness and resilience. Just get on with it. A good friend of mine used to carry around a coffee cup that said: Non Carborundum Illegitimis (don't let the bastards wear you down). This was his tribute to the people (and certain individuals in particular) who were giving him grief, but he never let them impact his work.

- **Deal with it.** Instead of moaning about your misfortune, figure out a solution. Think of where we'd be if Thomas Edison had just complained about being in the dark instead of inventing the light bulb. Change and hardships are opportunities in disguise. Use them to your advantage.

- **Don't let circumstances or people beyond your control change you for the worse.**

A story comes to mind of a man who was unfailingly polite to another man in his village who continued to ignore him. "Why do you always say 'Good morning' to him?" someone asked. "He never acknowledges you." "If I didn't, I'd be just as rude as he is," he replied. "I'm not going to let his rudeness impact my good manners."

- **Don't let success go to your head.** The ancient Greeks had a saying, "Whom the gods will destroy, they first make proud." Don't fall into this trap. If you should, in fact, be blessed with great good fortune, either by divine intervention or hard work, don't get a swollen head. Remain open to new ideas and other people, or your success might be very short lived.

- **Know your own limits.** If you are spending more time coping with problems beyond your control than is reasonable, you might want to consider moving to another position or to another organization.

When we think about President Abraham Lincoln, considered by many to be the greatest president the United States has ever had, we rarely attribute his success to his ability to cope. Yet it was mastery of this one key facet that allowed Lincoln to not only successfully steer the United States through the Civil War, the most devastating conflict it ever faced, but to win a greater victory than just the war itself. It was, however, very tough going. Dissent and dissatisfaction reigned from the capitol to the battlefield.

After the disastrous battle at Fredericksburg, a soldier, in a letter home, wrote, "...my loyalty is growing weak...I am sick and tired of disaster and the fools that bring disaster upon us..."

"He [Lincoln] is ignorant, self-willed ...incompetent," said another.

And Lincoln, himself, acknowledged, "If there is a worse place than Hell, I am in it."[2]

Little did he know; the worst was yet to come.

In 1862, prompted by Salmon P. Chase, the Secretary of the Treasury, a radical wing of Republican senators met in caucus and essentially plotted a coup to reorganize the cabinet in an attempt to oust Lincoln's Secretary of State, William H. Seward. Chase had led them to believe that progress in the war was going slowly because of Seward's undue influence over the president. It was because of Seward, Chase told them, that certain war measures, including emancipation of slaves, black soldiers, and the appointment of anti-slavery generals, had not been implemented. The rivalry between Seward and Chase was no secret, but what was unknown was Chase's ambition. His ultimate goal was a presidential nomination for himself.

IT WAS ABRAHAM LINCOLN'S ABILITY TO COPE THAT ALLOWED HIM TO SUCCESSFULLY STEER THE UNITED STATES THROUGH THE CIVIL WAR AND TO WIN A GREATER VICTORY THAN JUST THE WAR ITSELF.

Lincoln was distraught by the pending coup. "What do these men want?" he asked a friend. "They wish to get rid of me, and sometimes I am more than half disposed to gratify them...We are now on the brink of destruction. It appears to me that the Almighty is against us."[3]

A lesser individual might have folded under the mounting pressure. But Lincoln did not. He pulled himself together and handled the affair in a manner that only served to strengthen his leadership. He met with the senators and listened politely. Unbeknownst to them, Seward had already tendered his resignation to Lincoln. Lincoln invited them back the next day and, with his entire cabinet on hand, excluding Seward, he defended his Secretary of State and corrected every one of their misassumptions. Lincoln then turned to his cabinet for confirmation and a much-chagrined Chase was forced to mumble assent. Later he offered his resignation, but neither his nor Seward's resignation was accepted by the president.

Lincoln had no military training, yet he took a very hands-on interest in the conduct of the war and was generally unhappy about the Union's progress. His major complaint was that even though the Union Army had more troops, more munitions, and more food than the enemy, they never pursued the enemy when the tide of battle favored the North. Even when General Lee was soundly defeated at Gettysburg, General Meade made no attempt to prevent Lee and his army from retreating all the way across the Potomac River and into Virginia, their "home base."

Meade, who had lost many of his officers during the battle, knew his army was exhausted and feared that Lee might still be able to deliver a deadly counterattack. But Lincoln wanted to end the war and as much as he appreciated Meade's victory, he felt the general had let the enemy escape.

Lincoln coped with his disappointment by writing Meade a letter:

> As you had learned that I was dissatisfied, I have thought it best to kindly tell you why. I am very—*very*—grateful to you for the magnificent success you gave the cause of the country at Gettysburg; and I am sorry now to be the author of the slightest pain to you…Again my dear general, I do not believe you appreciate the magnitude of the misfortune involved in Lee's escape. He was within your easy grasp, and to have closed upon him would, in connection with our other late successes, have ended the war. As it is, the war will be prolonged indefi-nitely …Your golden opportunity is gone, and I am distressed immeasurably because of it.[4]

Then he put the letter in an envelope and tucked it away in his desk.

Meade never saw it.

The letter was Lincoln's way of coping with his huge disappointment. As satisfying as it might have been to send, it would not undo what had been done.

When the North first waged war with the South, it was with the idea of preserving the Union. As the war progressed, however, Lincoln saw an opportunity for a greater good and issued the Emancipation Proclamation. Hostility reigned again, not just from the South, but from Northerners as well.

"Monstrous, impudent and heinous," declared one Northern editorial. "Insulting to God as to man, for it declares those 'equal' whom God created unequal."

"Are you, as soldiers, bound by patriotism, duty or loyalty to fight in such a cause?" wrote another.[5]

As a result, so many members of two southern Illinois regiments deserted (rather than risk their lives to free the slaves), that General Grant had to disband the regiments. Yet Lincoln held firm. So much grief, destruction and loss of life had to account for something of greater value than just preserving the Union. As a result he was able to bring to a close the issue of slavery, which had plagued the founding fathers a hundred years prior and was still unresolved. The war, as horrific as it was, offered an opportunity. Lincoln seized it.

The trials and tribulations of our daily lives pale in comparison to those overcome by Shackleton and Lincoln. Yet if we can harness just a fragment of their ability to cope and apply it to our daily lives, we, too, can find, secure and hold on to success. If we do, another challenge awaits us.

Let's just suppose that nothing goes wrong in your life. You work hard, follow the rules, and attain riches and adoration of the kind you never dreamed possible. Now you have to learn to cope with that. You may have to cope with the press, or with people who want to borrow from you or just want a little bit of your success to rub off on them.

You might start to think that your way is the right way and that you are the only person with good ideas. That's when arrogance and pride, always lurking nearby, can badly tarnish your work and your reputation. By all means, and with best wishes, I hope you are fortunate, but be prepared to cope with what good fortune might bring!

───────────────

Ask Yourself: How am I coping? If you are having trouble coping, read the fundamentals again and find a way to cope or exit your job.

[1] Sir Ernest Shackleton, "South: the *Endurance* Expedition" (New York: New American Library, 1999).

[2] James M. McPherson, "Battle Cry of Freedom: The Civil War Era" (New York: Oxford University Press, 1988).

[3] Ibid.

[4] Stephen W. Sears, "Gettysburg" (New York: Houghton Mifflin Company, 2003).

[5] James M. McPherson, "Battle Cry of Freedom: The Civil War Era" (New York: Oxford University Press, 1988).

JUST DO YOUR BEST

And so, we've come to a close. I've shown you what successful people do and have listed the fundamental tasks that you need to do. The rest is up to you.

If nothing else, I hope you see that doing well doesn't necessarily demand that you do more. To achieve success you don't have to keep taking on more and more responsibility. You simply have to do the very best you can, all the time.

Believe that everything you do can be done better. The power of positive thinking should never be underestimated. Nor should the power of negative thinking.

Make sure you are meeting your job requirements, your major objectives and your daily and weekly assignments.

Periodically ask yourself: How am I doing on **knowing**? How am I doing on **deciding**? How am I doing on **assigning**? How am I doing on **influencing**? How am I doing on **coping**?

Critique your own performance. Compare it to the best that others have done in your position, and look for ways to improve.

Listen, talk and observe, but mostly listen and observe. There's a reason you have two ears and two eyes, but only one mouth.

Find a mentor or role model, coach or confidant. Read. Go to school. Study. Practice.

Help others.

Find inspiration, direction and ideas in the life stories of successful people. If there are some you want to emulate, then look for ways to do so.

Believe in yourself and enjoy the satisfaction derived from doing your best all day, every day.

INDEX

ABOUT THE AUTHOR
CHUCK HARWOOD

Part-time/Vacation Work:

vegetable farm worker, grocery delivery boy, camp counselor, shipping clerk, door-to-door cookware party salesperson

Education:

Concord, Massachusetts schools, Phillips Exeter Academy, Harvard University (BA, MBA)

Full-Time Positions Held:

shift foreperson, general foreperson, budget analyst, chief plant accountant, sales and marketing manager, division manager (vice-president), company president, company founder, consultant/teacher, author

Business Experience:

television picture tube glass, electronic components, laboratory products, glass products (international), integrated circuits, consulting and teaching

Full-Time Employers:

Corning, Inc., Signetics, Philips Electronics, The Quality Improvement Company

Volunteer Work:

church committees, leader of youth groups, president of a local United Way, various industry and not-for-profit boards and committees, pro bono consulting and teaching

Family:

one wife, six children, 16 grandchildren

Author:

"Kick Down the Door of Complacency: Seize the Power of Continuous Improvement", by Charles C. Harwood, St Lucie Press, 1998 www.conquercomplacency.com

NOTES

NOTES

Executive Search Leader

I find this book to be relevant for all levels of workers—from an apprentice to the seasoned CEO who needs a reminder. I would recommend this book to everyone—particularly to young people just starting out.

David L. Powell, Sr., Principal
David Powell, Inc.

Money Manager

Just Do Your Best is more than a practical, how-to book for job success. Motivated by an old-fashioned value system of self-reliance, courage, and courtesy, the author outlines a straightforward checklist for becoming a responsible adult. Peppered with easy-to-understand examples, this book should be required reading for upwardly mobile people between 5 and 105, starting with my four kids.

Tom Steyer, Principal
Farallon Capital Management

Chief Executive Officer, Manufacturing Firm

Here is a much-needed new approach for personal success. It's for everyone—but essential for those starting their first jobs or moving into new jobs.

Arthur W. Zafiropoulo
Chairman & C.E.O.
Ultratech, Inc.

Human Resources Executive

Having been in the human resources field my entire career, I have found that regardless of a person's education or discipline, the attribute most needed in business to succeed is common sense. This small book is big on common sense and wisdom for people in all kinds of jobs and professions.

Sandi Kile, Vice President, Human
Resources,
Fujitsu Microelectronics America

Police Officer

When I was assigned to work with gangs, I received special training and gained knowledge from the gangs on how they operate. I decided how to deploy my meager resources. I gave and received assignments. I influenced my chief and community leaders to do more. I coped with the slowness of everyone's response to the call for action. This book would have definitely helped me do things better and faster.

David Lanier, Police Lieutenant
Fremont, California

Organization and Development Professional

This book reframes the challenge of coping with events outside one's control, in an inspiring fashion that enables and empowers folks to succeed.

Richard J. Lee, Owner
Private Consulting Business

Author, Best Selling Business Books

From ranching to Shackleton exploring Antarctica. From marketing to Rachael Carson fighting to save the planet. These efforts and more define work at its best. This is an important book for just about everyone. It's short. It's well written. It's useful. If you follow even some of its guidelines, you will like your job better, and you will do better.

Bob Waterman, Co-author,
In Search of Excellence

Business School Professor

Success rarely comes from what we do alone. This book offers excellent tips for how you can gain influence beyond your authority or prescribed job. It offers a list of dos that are easy to understand and incorporate into your repertoire of personal skills.

Michael Beer, Cahners-Robb
Professor of Business
Administration, Emeritus
Harvard Business School

President/CEO

If a person's goal is to do his or her best (and it should be), they couldn't find a better book to help them.

Kathy Riggins, President/CEO
YMCA of the Mid-Peninsula
Northern California